P9-CCR-469

A gift for:

DONNA Miller

From:

Jim Miller

2-14-2016

The Joy of a Sacred Marriage
Copyright © 2007 by Gary Thomas
ISBN 978-0-310-81741-3

Excerpts taken from: *Sacred Marriage*. Copyright © 2000 by Gary L. Thomas. Published by Zondervan.

Excerpts taken from: *Devotions for a Sacred Marriage*. Copyright © 2005 by Gary L. Thomas. Published by Zondervan.

All Scripture quotations, unless otherwise noted, are taken from the Holy Bible: New International Version ®, (North American Edition). Copyright © 1973, 1978, 1984, by International Bible Society. Used by permission of Zondervan. All rights reserved.

The "NIV" and "New International Version" trademarks are registered in the United States Patent and Trademark Office by International Bible Society.

Scriptures marked MSG are from *The Message*. Copyright © by Eugene H. Peterson 1993, 1994, 1995, 1996, 2000, 2001, 2002. Used by permission of NavPress Publishing Group.

All rights reserved. No part of this publication may be reproduced, stored in a retrieval system, or transmitted in any form or by any means—electronic, mechanical, photocopy, recording, or any other—except for brief quotations in printed reviews, without the prior permission of the publisher.

Requests for information should be addressed to:
Inspirio, the gift group of Zondervan
Grand Rapids, Michigan 49530
www.inspiriogifts.com

Compiler: Robin Schmitt
Project Manager: Kim Zeilstra
Design Manager: Michael J. Williams
Production Manager: Matt Nolan
Designer: Robin Black, Blackbird Creative, www.blackbirdcreative.biz
Cover image: PhotoDisc

Printed in China
07 08 09/ 3 2 1

The Joy of a
SACRED
Marriage

GARY L. THOMAS

inspirio®

Introduction

Dear Readers:

Since the release of *Sacred Marriage*, I have had many requests
for a format that could be given as a wedding gift. Out of your
suggestions, this book was born. *The Joy of Sacred Marriage*
contains excerpts from both *Sacred Marriage* and *Devotions for a
Sacred Marriage* so that newlyweds can grasp the most important
and relevant topics without needing to sit down and read a whole
chapter. My hope is that this book will touch the lives of the newly
married, giving them an entirely new outlook on the depth and
meaning of Christian marriage.

The peace of Christ,
Gary

SACRED *Marriage*

Makes Us Holy

This book looks at how we can use the challenges, joys, struggles, and celebrations of marriage to draw closer to God and to grow in Christian character.

To spiritually benefit from marriage, we have to be honest. We have to look at our disappointments, own up to our ugly attitudes, and confront our selfishness. We also have to rid ourselves of the notion that the difficulties of marriage can be overcome if we simply pray harder or learn a few simple principles. Most of us have discovered that these "simple steps" work only on a superficial level. Why? Because there's a deeper question that needs to be addressed beyond how we can "improve" our marriage: What if God didn't design marriage to be "easier"? What if God had an end in mind that went beyond our happiness?

What if God designed marriage to make us holy more than to make us happy?

❄

We can use the challenges,

joys, struggles,

and celebrations of marriage

to draw closer to God

and to grow in

Christian character.

R omantic love," which is so celebrated in movies, songs, and cheap paperbacks, was virtually unknown to the ancients. There were exceptions, but taken as a whole, the concept that marriage should involve passion and fulfillment and excitement is a relatively recent development on the scale of human history.

This is *not* to suggest that romance itself or the desire for more romance is necessarily bad; good marriages work hard to preserve a sense of romance. But the idea that a marriage can survive on romance alone, or that romantic *feelings* are more important than any other consideration when choosing a spouse, has wrecked many a marital ship.

Romantic love has no elasticity to it. It can never be stretched; it simply shatters. Mature love, the kind demanded of a good marriage, *must* stretch.

Any mature, spiritually sensitive view of marriage must be built on the foundation of mature love rather than romanticism.

The romantic roller coaster of courtship eventually evens out to the terrain of a Midwest interstate. When this happens, couples respond in different ways. Many will break up their relationship and try to recreate the passionate romance with someone else. Other couples will descend into a sort of marital guerrilla warfare, a passive-aggressive power play as each partner blames the other for personal dissatisfaction or lack of excitement. Some couples decide to simply "get along." Still others may opt to pursue a deeper meaning, a spiritual truth hidden in the enforced intimacy of the marital situation.

We can run from the challenges of marriage, or we can admit that every marriage presents these challenges and asks us to address them head-on. We can discover in the challenges of marriage the opportunities to learn more about God, grow in our understanding of him, and learn to love him more.

*In all things God works
for the good of those who love him,
who have been called according to his purpose.
For those God foreknew he also predestined
to be conformed to the likeness of his Son.*

ROMANS 8:28–29

*Just as [God] who called you is holy,
so be holy in all you do;
for it is written:
"Be holy, because I am holy."*

1 PETER 1:15–16

I remember my brother asking me a few questions about what marriage was like. I thought for a moment and said, "If you want to be free to serve Jesus, there's no question—stay single. Marriage takes a lot of time. But if you want to become more like Jesus, I can't imagine any better thing to do than to get married. Being married forces you to face some character issues you'd never have to face otherwise."

The real transforming work of marriage is the twenty-four-hours-a-day, seven-days-a-week commitment. This is the crucible that grinds and shapes us into the character of Jesus Christ. Instead of getting up at 3:00 A.M. to begin prayer in a monastery, the question becomes, "Who will wake up when the baby's diaper needs changing?"

Marriage calls us to an entirely new and selfless life. And any situation that calls me to confront my selfishness has enormous spiritual value.

If you want to be free to serve Jesus,

there's no question — stay single.

Marriage takes a lot of time.

But if you want to become more like Jesus,

I can't imagine any better thing to do

than to get married.

Marriage is temporary in the light of eternity. The truth is, Lisa's and my relationship with God will outlive our marriage.

For the Christian, marriage is a penultimate rather than an ultimate reality. Because of this, both of us can find even more meaning by pursuing God together and by recognizing that he is the one who alone can fill the spiritual ache in our souls. We can work at making our home life more pleasant and peaceable; we can explore ways to keep sex fresh and fun; we can make superficial changes that will preserve at least the appearance of respect and politeness. But what both of us crave more than anything else is to be intimately close to the God who made us. If *that* relationship is right, we won't make such severe demands on our marriage, asking each other, expecting each other, to compensate for spiritual emptiness.

Spiritual growth is the main theme; marriage is simply the context. Just as celibates use abstinence and religious hermits use isolation, so we can use marriage for the same purpose—to grow in our service, obedience, character, pursuit, and love of God.

You've probably already realized that there was a purpose for your marriage that went beyond happiness. You might not have chosen the word *holiness* to express it, but you understood there was a transcendent truth beyond the superficial romance depicted in popular culture. We're going to explore that purpose.

The ultimate purpose of this book is not to make you love your spouse more—although I think that will happen along the way. It is to equip you to love your God more and to help you reflect the character of his Son more precisely.

*Praise be to the God and Father of
our Lord Jesus Christ, who has blessed us in the heavenly
realms with every spiritual blessing in Christ.
For he chose us in him before the creation of the world
to be holy and blameless in his sight.*

EPHESIANS 1:3 – 4

*We, who with unveiled faces all reflect the
Lord's glory, are being transformed into his likeness
with ever-increasing glory, which comes
from the Lord, who is the Spirit.*

2 CORINTHIANS 3:18

15

Teaches Us About God

One aspect of the marital experience—cooperating with God to bring children into being—should be particularly meaningful for Christians. The picture of God as Creator is central to his authority, identity, and purpose. In fact, the Bible is framed around the fact that God is Creator. The first thing we learn about God in the book of Genesis is that he created the heavens and the earth (see Genesis 1:1); the last image of the New Testament shows God creating a new heaven and a new earth.

This is just one of several analogies that connect various aspects of marriage with our understanding of God. A giant thread runs throughout Scripture comparing God's relationship to his people with the human institution of marriage. These various analogies use the experience of marriage to teach us valuable truths about the nature of God.

In that day," declares the LORD,
  "you will call me 'my husband';
  you will no longer call me 'my master.'
I will betroth you to me forever;
  I will betroth you in righteousness and justice,
  in love and compassion."

HOSEA 2:16, 19

As a bridegroom rejoices over his bride,
  so will your God rejoice over you.

ISAIAH 62:5

For Christians seeking to gain spiritual insight from their marriage, analogies between the marital union and various mysteries of faith provide the necessary ingredients for serious, contemplative reflection. God did not create marriage just to give us a pleasant means of repopulating the world and providing a steady societal institution for the benefit of humanity. He planted marriage among humans as yet another signpost pointing to his own eternal, spiritual existence.

As humans with finite minds, we need the power of symbolism to gain understanding. By means of the simple relationship of a man and a woman, the symbol of marriage can call up virtually infinite meaning. This will happen only when we use our marriage to *explore* God. If we are consumed with highlighting where our spouses are falling short, we will miss the divine mysteries of marriage and the lessons it has to teach us.

God planted marriage among humans

as yet another signpost pointing

to his own eternal, spiritual existence.

Will we approach marriage from a God-centered view or a man-centered view? In a man-centered view, we will maintain our marriage as long as our earthly comforts, desires, and expectations are met. In a God-centered view, we preserve our marriage because it brings glory to God.

Both the Old and New Testaments use marriage as a central analogy—the union between God and Israel (Old Testament) and the union between Christ and his church (New Testament). Understanding the depth of these analogies is crucial, as they will help us determine the very foundation on which a truly Christian marriage is based. If I believe the primary purpose of marriage is to model God's love for his church, I will enter this relationship and maintain it with an entirely new motivation: "to please him" (2 Corinthians 5:9).

THE GOD-CENTERED SPOUSE

Let us purify ourselves from everything that contaminates body and spirit, perfecting holiness out of reverence for God.

2 CORINTHIANS 7:1

Are you a God-centered spouse or a spouse-centered spouse? A spouse-centered spouse acts nicely toward her husband when he acts nicely toward her. She is accommodating, as long as her husband pays her attention. A spouse-centered husband will go out of his way for his wife, as long as she remains agreeable and affectionate. He'll romance her, as long as he feels rewarded for doing so.

But Paul tells us we are to perfect holiness *out of reverence for God*. Since God is always worthy to be revered, we are always called to holiness; we are always called to love. A God-centered spouse feels more motivated by his or her commitment to God than by whatever response a spouse may give.

21

The first purpose in marriage—beyond happiness, sexual expression, the bearing of children, companionship, mutual care and provision, or anything else—is to please God. Paul underscores it: "Those who live should no longer live for themselves but for him who died for them and was raised again" (2 Corinthians 5:15). I owe it to Jesus Christ to live for him, to make him my consuming passion and the driving force in my life.

The very nature of Christ's work was a reconciling work, bringing us together again with God. Our response is to become reconcilers ourselves. Everything I do is to be supportive of this "ministry of reconciliation" (v. 18), and that begins by displaying reconciliation in my personal relationships, especially in my marriage.

If my "driving force" is as it should be, I will work to construct a marriage that enhances this ministry of reconciliation—a marriage that incarnates this truth by putting flesh on it, building a relationship that models forgiveness, selfless love, and sacrifice.

The first purpose in marriage—

beyond happiness, sexual expression,

the bearing of children, companionship,

mutual care and provision, or anything else—

is to please God.

One of the reasons the trees on the western slope of the Cascades survive so long is simple: The Washington forests are so wet that lightning strikes cause relatively few fires. Lightning strikes still come but they're not as devastating, so trees have a longer time to take root and grow.

That's a good picture of a marriage based on the ministry of reconciliation. Strong Christian marriages will still be struck by lightning—sexual temptation, communication problems, frustrations, unrealized expectations—but if the marriages are heavily watered with an unwavering commitment to please God above everything else, the conditions won't be ripe for a devastating fire to follow the lightning strike.

If I'm married only for happiness, and my happiness wanes for whatever reason, one little spark will burn the entire forest of my relationship. But if my aim is to proclaim and model God's ministry of reconciliation, my endurance will be fireproof.

*All this is from God, who reconciled us to himself
through Christ and gave us the ministry of reconciliation:
that God was reconciling the world to himself
in Christ, not counting men's sins against them.
And he has committed to us the message of reconciliation.
We are therefore Christ's ambassadors,
as though God were making his appeal through us.*

2 CORINTHIANS 5:18 – 20

Teaches Us to Love

Someone once asked Jesus what the greatest commandment was, and he replied that there were two (Matthew 22:34–40). It wasn't enough to love God with all your heart, soul, mind, and strength. If you really wanted to please God, Jesus said, you must love others.

Marriage can be the gym in which our capacity to experience and express God's love is strengthened and further developed. To get there, we have to realize that human love and divine love aren't two separate oceans but rather one body of water with many tributaries. We show our love for God in part by loving our spouses well.

Marriage creates a climate where this love is put to the greatest test. The problem is that love must be *acquired*. Love is not a natural response that gushes out of us unbidden. Infatuation sometimes does that—at first—but Christian love must be chased after, aspired to, and practiced.

Marriage can be the gym

in which our capacity to experience

and express God's love is strengthened

and further developed.

✻

Christian love is displayed in loving the most difficult ones to love. That's what's so difficult about Jesus' call to love others. On one level, it's easy to love God, because God doesn't have bad breath. God doesn't reward kindness with evil. But Jesus really let us have it when he attached our love for God with our love for other people.

In the marriage context, we have no excuse. God lets us *choose* whom we're going to love. What grounds do we have to ever stop loving? If I can't love my wife, how can I love the homeless man? Yes, this spouse might be difficult to love at times, but that's what marriage is for — *to teach us how to love.*

Allow your marriage relationship to enlarge your capacity for love — to teach you to be a Christian. Use marriage as a practice court, where you learn to accept others and serve them.

Young men in Israel were called to serve God by fighting wars, except for a bridegroom: "For one year he is to ... stay at home and bring happiness to [his] wife" (Deuteronomy 24:5). God wants me to serve him by making my wife happy!

Every spouse should spend time thinking about how to make their spouse happy—and celebrating the profound reality that doing so pleases God. A husband who plots how to make his wife laugh now and then is serving God. A wife who plans an unforgettable sexual experience for her husband is serving God. A husband who makes sacrifices so his wife can get the recreational time she needs is loving God.

When Jesus said, "Love the Lord your God ... love your neighbor," he opened up the vistas of love and removed the walls that encase us. He made divine love and "religion" much bigger than we realize.

Jesus said, "'Love the Lord your God
with all your heart and with
all your soul and with all your mind.'
This is the first and greatest commandment.
And the second is like it:
'Love your neighbor as yourself.'"

MATTHEW 22:37 – 39

These three remain: faith, hope and love.
But the greatest of these is love.

1 CORINTHIANS 13:13

A PRAYER TO REMEMBER

Be imitators of God, therefore,
as dearly loved children and live a life of love,
just as Christ loved us and gave himself up for us
as a fragrant offering and sacrifice to God.

EPHESIANS 5:1 – 2

I am called to be the one person so devoted to my wife's overall good that I commit myself to being there on her behalf, regardless of any disappointments or faults. Imagine how your marriage might change if you spent some time praying, "Lord, how can I love him [or her] today like he [or she] has never been loved?" The answer may be very practical: take over a chore, speak a word of encouragement, or take care of something that needs fixing. Or it may be romantic, or over-the-top creative, or generous, or very simple.

❋

Imagine how your marriage might change if,

before your spouse returned home this evening,

you spent some time asking God — and listening for

his response — "Lord, how can I love him [or her]

today like he [or she] has never been loved?"

Your spouse seems so unlike you. You ask yourself, "How can I possibly love someone so different from me?" Yet how could you possibly love God? He is spirit, and you're encased in flesh. He is eternal, and you're trapped in time. He is holy, and you're imperfect. It is far less of a leap for one person to love another than it is for either to love God.

Marriage is designed to call us out of ourselves and learn to love the "different." Put together in the closest situation imaginable, we are forced to respect and appreciate someone so radically different.

We need to be called out of ourselves because we are incomplete. God made us to find our fulfillment in him—the Totally Other. Marriage shows us we are not all there is; it calls us to give way to another but also to find joy, happiness, and even ecstasy in another.

There are no lessons to be learned when a husband dominates his wife. There are no inspiring examples to emulate when a wife manipulates a husband. But love unlocks the spiritual secrets of the universe. Love blows open eternity and showers its raindrops on us.

Christianity involves believing certain things, to be sure, but its herald, its hallmark, its glory is not in merely ascribing to certain intellectual truths. The beauty of Christianity is in learning to love, and few life situations test that so radically as does a marriage.

Yes, it is difficult to love your spouse. But if you truly want to love God, look right now at the ring on your left hand, and commit yourself to exploring anew what that ring represents and love passionately, crazily, and enduringly the fleshly person who put it there.

It just may be one of the most spiritual things you can do.

Love is patient, love is kind.

It does not envy, it does not boast, it is not proud.

It is not rude, it is not self-seeking,

it is not easily angered, it keeps no record of wrongs.

Love does not delight in evil but rejoices with the truth.

It always protects, always trusts, always hopes,

always perseveres. Love never fails.

1 CORINTHIANS 13:4 – 8

35

Teaches Us to Respect Others

Few Christians think of giving respect as a command or a spiritual discipline. We're obsessed with *being* respected but rarely consider our obligation to respect others. Yet Scripture makes this obligation clear: "Show proper respect to everyone" (1 Peter 2:17).

When our desire for respect isn't met, we're tempted to lapse into a self-defeating response. Rather than work to earn respect, we work to tear down our spouse in a desperate attempt to convince ourselves that their lack of respect is meaningless. Spiritually, this becomes a vicious, debilitating cycle that's difficult to break.

God has a solution that, if we adopt it, will revolutionize our relationships. While many people fight to *receive* respect, Christian marriage calls us to focus our efforts on *giving* respect. We're called to honor someone even when we know their deepest character flaws. We're called to learn to respect this person with whom we've become so familiar.

While many people fight

to *receive* respect,

Christian marriage calls us

to focus our efforts on *giving* respect.

Mark Twain tells the sobering tale about deeply exploring the Mississippi River he loved so much. He found that the river had lost much of its poetry. The mystery of that mighty waterway had been replaced with a boring predictability.

As our partners become more familiar to us, respect often becomes harder to give. But this is a sign of spiritual immaturity more than an inevitable pathway of marriage. Consider Paul as he wrote to the Corinthians. He was familiar with all their faults, yet he continued to be thankful for them. Why? "Because of [God's] grace given you in Christ Jesus" (1 Corinthians 1:4).

As C. J. Mahaney so eloquently explains it, we can be thankful for our fellow sinners when we spend more time looking for "evidences of grace" than we do finding fault. Giving respect is an act of maturity, birthed in a profound understanding of God's good grace.

Genesis 1:27 teaches that both male *and* female are made in God's image. This calls me to a far more noble response than simply refraining from being condescending to my wife. Her creation in God's image calls me to honor her.

As my family went through the National Gallery of Art, one of my children reached out to touch a painting. My wife grabbed our child's hand with a harsh whisper. "This is a *Rembrandt*!"

My wife was created by God himself! How dare I dishonor her? In fact, shouldn't it even give me pause before I reach out to touch her? She is the Creator's daughter!

Giving respect to others brings light and life into our lives. It leads us to respect the God who created all of us and shapes us as he sees fit. It's an essential discipline, and marriage provides daily opportunities for us to grow in this area.

*There is neither . . . male nor female,
for you are all one in Christ Jesus.*

GALATIANS 3:28

*Husbands . . . be considerate
as you live with your wives,
and treat them with respect.*

1 PETER 3:7

*Each one of you also must love his wife as he loves himself,
and the wife must respect her husband.*

EPHESIANS 5:33

I spent the first few years of my marriage adding up my pluses and my wife's minuses. Then one morning a question startled me: "Does Lisa feel like she's married to Jesus?"

I'm told in Scripture that my duty as a Christian is to become like Christ. Over time, my spouse should start to feel like there's at least a family resemblance.

"But wait!" the selfish me wanted to cry out. "What about *her*?" I began thinking about how my wife could improve, but then I remembered a passage written by William Law: "No one is of the Spirit of Christ but he that has the utmost compassion for sinners...."

When my respect slips into contempt, it's because *I'm* weak, not because my wife is failing. If I were really mature, I'd have the same compassion for her weaknesses as Christ does. Respect is a spiritual discipline, an obligation that I owe my wife.

My duty as a Christian is

to become like Christ.

Over time, my spouse should start to feel

like there's at least a family resemblance.

My wife and I entered a new journey together when I began working out of our home. Other married couples were amazed. "And you still *like* each other?"

Actually, it did wonders for our marriage. We developed a profound appreciation for what the other person was doing. Both of us now understand more clearly the challenges facing each of us and why it's sometimes so hard to act like the perfect partner. We're not married in a carefree Garden of Eden. We're married in the midst of many responsibilities that compete for our energy. This new understanding ushered in a stronger empathy for each other in our weaknesses and peculiarities.

Instead of focusing your energy on resentment over how sparsely your spouse understands you, strive to understand him or her. Find out what your spouse's day is really like. Take time to do an inventory of your spouse's difficulties rather than your spouse's shortcomings.

KEEPING THE FOCUS WHERE IT BELONGS

*First take the plank out of your eye, and then you
will see clearly to remove the speck from your brother's eye.*

LUKE 6:42

When you pray for your spouse, how do you sound to God? Are
you spending more time asking how you can love your spouse like
he or she has never been or ever will be loved, or are you endlessly
repeating your spouse's failures and presenting God with a laundry
list of things you want changed?

If God seems silent, maybe he's hoping you'll turn the mirror
on yourself. Revolutionize your marriage by asking God where
you fall short. When you're tempted to turn the spotlight on your
spouse, ask for God's gentle correction: "Lord, where am I falling
short of your will for me to be a loving husband [wife]? Where do
I need to grow? Am I loving my spouse with the extravagant love
displayed by Jesus?"

✻

44

Thanksgiving is both a privilege and an obligation: "Give thanks in all circumstances" (1 Thessalonians 5:18). When I'm thankful for my spouse, the control that the familiarity of contempt has on me is broken. I look for new things to be thankful for. I try not to take the routine things she does for granted. I never eat at somebody's house without thanking them for providing a meal; why shouldn't I give my wife the same thanks?

There are few things that lift my spirits more than hearing my wife or children say, "Thanks for working so hard to provide for us." Those nine words can lift a hundred pounds of pressure off my back.

Contempt is conceived with expectations. Respect is conceived with expressions of gratitude. We can choose which one we'll obsess over—expectations, or thanksgivings. That choice will result in a birth—and the child will be named either contempt or respect.

45

Fosters Good Prayer

When Peter says men must be considerate of their wives and treat them with respect *so nothing will hinder their prayers* (1 Peter 3:7), he's directly connecting our attitude toward our wives with *the* fundamental Christian discipline.

The rules changed when I got married. A condition was placed on my prayer life, and that condition is tied directly to how I view and treat my wife.

I will never again be able to approach prayer "as if" I were a single man. God sees me, in one sense, through my wife. This means that if I want to grow as a married pray-er, I can't make believe I'm a celibate monk.

In fact, much Christian teaching has gotten it exactly backwards. We're told that if we want to have a stronger marriage, we should improve our prayer lives. But Peter tells us *we should improve our marriages so we can improve our prayer lives.*

Instead of prayer being the "tool"

that will refine my marriage,

marriage is the tool

that will refine my prayers!

J im Murphy, an associate pastor at my church, wouldn't make anyone's almanac of "distinguished national Christian leaders." But he may be one of the most godly men I know.

I was particularly moved when I heard Jim's wife say in his absence, "Jim is a saint. He really is." With these seven words she preached one of the most challenging sermons I've ever heard. I'm still trying to live up to Jim's example.

So, men, ask yourselves: "Do I respect my wife?" If prayer has been a problem area for you, this could be the first place to look for some answers to why you've been having difficulties. Ask your wife: "Am I considerate of you?" Encourage her to be honest.

If you want to grow toward God, you must build a stronger prayer life. If you're married, to attain a stronger prayer life you must learn to respect your spouse and be considerate.

GOD'S SON, GOD'S DAUGHTER

Can a mother forget the baby at her breast
and have no compassion on the child she has borne?
Though she may forget, I will not forget you!
See, I have engraved you on the palms of my hands.

ISAIAH 49:15 – 16

When I realized I'm married to *God's daughter*, everything about how I view marriage changed overnight. It was no longer about just me and one other person; it was very much a relationship with a passionately interested third partner. We've been encouraged to contemplate the Fatherhood of God, a wonderful and true doctrine. But if you want to change your marriage, spend some time thinking about God as Father-*in-Law*.

When I fail to respect my wife, I'm courting trouble with the heavenly Father, who feels passionately about my spouse's welfare. Never forget: you didn't just marry a man or a woman; you married God's son or God's daughter. Treat him or her accordingly.

There's another aspect of marriage that greatly affects my prayer life: unresolved disputes. Jesus said, "If you are offering your gift at the altar and there remember that your brother has something against you, leave your gift there in front of the altar. First go and be reconciled to your brother; then come and offer your gift" (Matthew 5:23–24).

Here is a picture of someone approaching God in prayer. As she kneels, she remembers that things aren't right between her and somebody else. Before she continues praying, her energies should be directed on reconciling with that other person—who could, of course, be her spouse. God hates dissension (see Proverbs 6:19) and treasures unity (see Psalm 133:1).

Marriage can force us to become stronger people, because if we want to maintain a strong prayer life as married partners, we must learn how to forgive. We must become expert reconcilers.

How wonderful, how beautiful,
when brothers and sisters get along!

PSALM 133:1 MSG

Jesus said, "When you stand praying,
if you hold anything against anyone, forgive him, so that
your Father in heaven may forgive you your sins."

MARK 11:25

51

I t's easy to get along with people if you never get close to them. I could undoubtedly allow a certain immaturity to remain in my life as a single man, choosing not to deal with my selfishness and judgmental spirit, "sidestepping" people who raise your blood pressure.

That option is obliterated in marriage. My wife and I live together every day. We're going to disagree about some things, and I'm unquestionably obligated to maintain my intimacy with her. When we face unrealized expectations, disappoint each other, or even maliciously wound each other, will we allow dissension—which God hates—to predominate, or will we do the necessary relational work to achieve unity?

Jesus makes it absolutely clear that you must choose unity if you want to maintain a vital prayer relationship with God. Dissension is a major prayer-killer. Marriage is designed to force us to become reconcilers. That's the only way we'll survive spiritually.

Jesus makes it absolutely clear

that you must choose unity if you want to maintain

a vital prayer relationship with God.

Marriage is a spotlight showing us that our search for another human being to "complete" us is misguided. When disillusionment breaks through, we have a choice: Dump our spouse and become infatuated with somebody new, or seek our significance, meaning, and purpose in our Creator rather than in another human being.

Approached correctly, marriage can cause us to reevaluate our dependency on other humans for our spiritual nourishment and direct us to nurture our relationship with God instead. No human being can love us the way we long to be loved; it's just not possible for another human to alleviate the spiritual ache God has placed in us all.

Marriage does us a great favor in exposing this truth, but it presents a corresponding danger—getting entangled in dissension. For the sake of prayer, it's essential that we live in unity. For the sake of unity, our passions and desires must be God-directed.

I f we connect our marital experience to our Christian faith, we can learn the power of prayer in new ways. By physically experiencing what it means to gently and lovingly caress my wife, perhaps I'll be able to understand new dimensions of prayer. How might God like to be touched and caressed? Can my verbal praises be like a hand lovingly stroking a cheek?

What I'm suggesting is that we connect our marriages with our faith in such a way that our experience in each feeds the other. Don't be afraid to use all aspects of marriage—even sexual expression—to expand your prayer life.

In many different ways marriage feeds into and builds our prayer lives. By learning to respect others, meeting each others' sexual needs, overcoming dissension, and using the analogies of marriage to foster more creative prayer, we can build and maintain active, growing, and meaningful prayer lives.

Exposes Our Sin

Early church leaders didn't necessarily consider celibacy a more difficult life than marriage. Some of the ancients realized that the marital life could be even *tougher* than the celibate life.

One night early in our marriage, I was astonished at my wife's endurance. She'd been up late with me, and later that night our children became ill. That night, being a celibate nun would have sounded like a dream vacation to Lisa.

It's probably not productive to argue either celibacy or marriage as the preferred pathway to holiness. Christians have walked both paths successfully. The important thing is to view the challenges of our particular life situation as a platform for growth. When marital challenges are faced head-on, our marriage can nurture our devotional lives in enriching ways. One of the ways is by unmasking our sin and our hurtful attitudes and thus leading us into the spirit of humility.

What marriage has done for me is hold up a mirror to my sin. It forces me to face myself honestly and consider my character flaws, selfishness, and anti-Christian attitudes, encouraging me to be sanctified and cleansed and to grow in godliness.

I always thought of myself as reasonably patient—until I got married and discovered how passionately annoyed I can become about empty ice-cube trays. It finally dawned on me that if it takes Lisa just seven seconds to fill one, *that's all it takes me as well.* Was I really so selfish that I was willing to let seven seconds' worth of inconvenience become a serious issue in my marriage?

Being so close to someone may be the greatest spiritual challenge in the world. This presupposes, of course, that I'm willing to be confronted with my sin. Do you hide from your spouse? Or do you utilize the spotlight of marriage to grow in grace?

What marriage has done for me

is hold up a mirror to my sin.

It forces me to face myself honestly and consider

my character flaws, selfishness, and

anti-Christian attitudes,

encouraging me to be sanctified and cleansed

and to grow in godliness.

I t is possible to enter marriage with a view to being cleansed spiritually, if, that is, we do so with a willingness to embrace marriage as a spiritual discipline. To do this, we must not enter marriage predominantly to be fulfilled, emotionally satisfied, or romantically charged, but rather to become more like Jesus Christ. We must embrace the reality of having our flaws exposed to our partner, and thereby having them exposed to us as well. Sin never seems quite as shocking when it is known only to us; when we see how it looks or sounds to another, it is magnified ten times over. The celibate can "hide" frustration by removing herself from the situation, but the married man or woman has no true refuge. It is hard to hide when you share the same bed.

Search me, O God, and know my heart;
    test me and know my anxious thoughts.
See if there is any offensive way in me,
    and lead me in the way everlasting.

PSALM 139:23 – 24

Have mercy on me, O God,
    according to your unfailing love;
according to your great compassion
    blot out my transgressions.
Wash away all my iniquity
    and cleanse me from my sin.

PSALM 51:1 – 2

I have a theory: Behind virtually every case of marital dissatisfaction lies unrepented sin. Couples don't fall out of love so much as they fall out of repentance. Sin, wrong attitudes, and personal failures that are not dealt with slowly erode the relationship, assaulting and eventually erasing the once lofty promises made in the throes of an earlier (and less-polluted) passion.

All of us enter marriage with sinful attitudes. When these attitudes surface, the temptation will be to hide them or even run to another relationship where the attitudes won't be so well known. But Christian marriage presumes a certain degree of self-disclosure. When I gave my hand in marriage, I committed to allow myself to be known by Lisa — and that means she'll see me as I am — with my faults, my prejudices, my fears, and my weaknesses.

Use the revelation of your sin as a means to grow in the foundational Christian virtue of humility, leading you to confession and renouncement. Then adopt the positive virtue that corresponds to the sin you are renouncing. If you've used women in the past, practice serving your wife. If you've been quick to ridicule your husband, practice giving him encouragement and praise.

View marriage as an entryway into sanctification—as a relationship that will reveal your sinful behaviors and attitudes and give you the opportunity to address them before the Lord. But here's the challenge: Don't give in to the temptation to resent your partner as your own weaknesses are revealed. Correspondingly, give them the freedom and acceptance they need in order to face their own weaknesses as well. In this way, we can use marriage as a leg up, a piercing spiritual mirror, designed for our sanctification and growth in holiness.

Viewing marriage as a doorway into sanctification points to another important principle—not just having my sin exposed, but reflecting on how I treat my wife when her sin is exposed. Do I use this knowledge to crush her, humiliate her, or gain power over her, or do I use it to gently and lovingly lead her into imitating the character of Jesus Christ?

Possessing the knowledge of someone's sin is a powerful and dangerous thing. In order for this discipline to work, we will have to link it with the discipline of forgiveness. This discipline of having our own sin exposed and being a spotlight for our spouse is a difficult one to master. It takes tremendous courage, and it takes what will seem (particularly to men) like an almost melodramatic gentleness. The marital relationship shouldn't be a "grilling" experience but rather a nurturing one—encouraging one another on the pathway of sanctification.

❈

LOVE MERCY

He has showed you, O man, what is good.
And what does the LORD require of you?
To act justly and to love mercy
and to walk humbly with your God.

MICAH 6.8

Because we married a sinner, we're going to see some ugly things. That's why our attitude toward another's sin will determine, in large part, the degree of intimacy we can achieve in marriage.

One glorious day, God used Micah 6:8 to open my eyes to a reality so large, it changed everything about how I view my marriage.

What does it mean to fall in love with mercy? It means I'm to become mercy's biggest fan. Having received mercy from God, I'm to walk in assurance and thankfulness, using my own gift of mercy as the lens through which I view anyone else's sin — including that of my spouse.

S eek to understand what a gift you've been given in God's
  mercy. From that foundation, explore the riches of extending
  this same mercy to others, beginning with your spouse.

Once when we looked at photographs we'd picked up at the
store, I realized how much weight I'd put on. My natural inclination
was to blame the camera angle.

The same thing happens with our sin in marriage. We resent the
revealed truth and are tempted to take it out on our spouse —
the camera, so to speak.

Much of our marital dissatisfaction stems from self-hatred.
We don't like what we've done or become; we've let selfish and sinful
attitudes poison our thoughts and lead us into shameful behaviors,
and suddenly all we want is *out*. The mature response isn't to leave;
it's to change — *ourselves*.

Whenever marital dissatisfaction rears its head, I simply check
my focus. The times that I'm happiest and most fulfilled in my
marriage are the times when I'm intent on drawing meaning and
fulfillment from becoming a better husband rather than from
demanding a "better" wife.

Teaches Us to Persevere

The relationship between God and his people was anything but easy. There were times of great joy and celebration, frustration and anger, infidelity and apostasy, and excruciating seasons of silence.

Sound like any relationship you know? Your own marriage, for example?

Viewed through this lens, the marriage relationship allows us to experientially identify with God and his relationship with Israel. Has your marriage had periods of joy and celebration? God can relate to and rejoice with you. Have you experienced the heartbreaking betrayal of unfaithfulness? Or the frustration of mournful silence? If so, you are not alone, and you've been given the raw materials with which to build a more intimate relationship with God.

One characteristic holds the history of God and Israel together—*perseverance*. When Israel turned her back on God, God didn't turn his back on Israel. He may have stepped back for a time, but the overall commitment remained concrete and steadfast.

Marriage helps us to develop the character of God himself as we stick with our spouses through the good times and the bad. Every wedding gives birth to a new history, a new beginning. The spiritual meaning of marriage is found in maintaining that history together.

When I hear of couples who break up after just three or four years, I feel sad because they haven't even begun to experience what being married is really like. It's like climbing halfway up a mountain but never getting to see the sights; you're in the middle of the task, your soul is consumed with the struggle, but it's much too soon to experience the full rewards. Becoming one — in the deepest, most intimate sense — takes time. It's a journey that never really ends, but it takes at least the span of a decade for the sense of intimacy to really display itself in the marriage relationship.

Marriage helps us to

develop the character of God himself

as we stick with our spouses

through the good times and the bad.

❋

rue Christian spirituality has always emphasized perseverance: "To those *who by persistence* in doing good seek glory, honor and immortality, he will give eternal life" (Romans 2:7, italics added).

Righteousness—true holiness—is seen *over time* in our persistence. It is relatively easy to "flirt" with righteousness—being occasionally courteous to other drivers (if you happen to be in a good mood), helping someone in need by opening the door for them (if you have time), throwing a few extra bucks into the offering plate (as long as you won't miss them). But this behavior is in reality superficial righteousness. The righteousness God seeks is a *persistent* righteousness, a commitment to continue making the right decision even when, perhaps hourly, you feel pulled in the opposite direction. Holiness is far more than an *inclination* toward occasional acts of kindness and charity. It is a commitment to persistent surrender before God.

Let us not become weary in doing good,

for at the proper time we will reap a harvest

if we do not give up.

GALATIANS 6:9

We also rejoice in our sufferings,

because we know that suffering produces perseverance;

perseverance, character; and character, hope.

ROMANS 5:3 – 4

W hat causes us to give up on our marriages? Although Jesus wasn't specifically addressing the marriage relationship in his parable of the sower, he covers many of the sources of our failure to persevere in marriage. Some of us give up when "the time of testing" comes (Luke 8:13). We thought marriage would be easy; when it gets hard, we bail out.

Others give up when they are choked by "life's worries" (Luke 8:14). Marriage counselors tell us that money problems have destroyed more marriages than just about anything else. There is also our selfishness and our sin—both of which are capable of polluting a once-precious affection.

What gives us the power to persist in doing good? Paul notes that in our persistence we seek "glory, honor and immortality" (Romans 2:7). These are words that point to an afterlife. Persistence doesn't make sense unless we live with a keen sense of eternity.

71

WORTH THE PAIN

Consider it pure joy, my brothers, whenever you face trials of many kinds, because you know that the testing of your faith develops perseverance. Perseverance must finish its work so that you may be mature and complete, not lacking anything.

JAMES 1:2 – 4

It's normal to go through difficult seasons and to occasionally fall into a funk. These are the gritty realities of real marriage. Don't kid yourself. Spiritual growth is not easy; it is about the most difficult exercise known to humankind. But please, don't give up! The perseverance these seasons produce is worth it.

Marriage can be difficult; spiritual growth can be exhausting— but they are worth the pain. In the end they produce a far-deeper life and a much-richer existence than living in a world of superficiality and throwaway relationships.

Christian endurance is based on the idea that there's another life, commonly known as heaven, which is eternal and for which this world is a preparation. The coming world is so glorious, weighted with so much honor, that it's worth making sacrifices now to receive glory, honor, and immortality there.

Around which world is your life centered? Your marriage will ultimately reveal the answer to that question. If we have an eternal outlook, preparing for eternity by sticking with a difficult marriage makes much more sense than destroying a family to gain quick and easy relief.

One of the most poetic lines in Scripture, one that I wish every husband and wife would display in a prominent place in their home, is found in 2 Thessalonians 3:5: "May the Lord direct your hearts into God's love and Christ's perseverance."

There's the Bible's best recipe for holiness and a "successful" life here on earth.

God's love and Christ's perseverance—

there's the Bible's best recipe for

holiness and a "successful" life here on earth.

Christmas Eve and Christmas morning are merely the climaxes to a long-running story set in motion centuries before. It's a fascinating tale, one that God follows with all the passion of an adoring husband. It would not be fair to judge that history at any one point, for it is the history of God and his people Israel—his bride and his spouse—taken together over the long run, that tells the complete story.

Learning to cherish my sacred history with Lisa has been one of the most spiritually meaningful practices in my life. We have created a history together that is enriching, meaningful, and laden with passion. Yes, we have had to travel through a few valleys to get to where we are. Yes, there were moments when the history seemed threatened, but if the journey had its difficulties, the sights along the way and our destination have been worth it.

Builds Our Character

There are few natural wonders more startling in their beauty than Mount Everest. Geologists believe that the Himalayas were created by the Indian continent crashing into Eurasia. "Crashing" is a writer's hyperbole; actually, the two continents collide with a movement of about ten centimeters per year. But slow and steady does the job. As India keeps moving inward, compressing and lifting southern Eurasia, a spectacular natural treasure continues to be created.

If there were no collision between India and Eurasia, there would be no Himalayas. Without the wrenching force of continental shifting, the world would be a poorer place aesthetically.

In the same way, the "collisions" of marriage can create relationships of beauty. Beauty is often birthed in struggle. These points of impact may not be "fun"—in fact, they can make us feel like we're being ripped apart—but the process can make us stronger, build our character, and deepen our faith.

*S*truggle makes us stronger; it builds us up and deepens our faith. But this result is achieved only when we face the struggle head-on, not when we run from it. Gary and Betsy Ricucci point out, "Our Lord has sovereignly ordained that our refining process take place as we go *through* difficulties, not around them. The Bible is filled with examples of those who overcame as they passed *through* the desert, the Red Sea, the fiery furnace, and ultimately the cross. God doesn't protect Christians from their problems—he helps them walk victoriously *through* their problems."

If your marriage is tough, get down on your knees and thank God that he has given you an opportunity for unparalleled spiritual growth. You have the prime potential to excel in Christian character and obedience.

Struggle makes us stronger;

it builds us up and deepens our faith.

But this result is achieved only when

we face the struggle head-on,

not when we run from it.

As a cross-country runner, my most satisfying victories were those that took every ounce of strength. In one race, the weather was hot and I set a bruising pace. I had to keep making a conscious decision not to quit. When I collapsed across the finish line, I was almost too tired to be elated over the win. I had given it my all, and there was a certain awe in that knowledge. It wasn't fun, but it was very *meaningful*.

God created us in such a way that we need to struggle to stay alive. Challenge keeps us seasoned. But to be profitable, our struggle must have *purpose* and must be *productive*. Two people who do nothing but fight in their marriage and make each other miserable aren't engaging in a helpful spiritual exercise. It's only when we put struggle within the Christian context of character development and self-sacrifice that it becomes profitable.

No discipline seems pleasant at the time,
but painful. Later on, however,
it produces a harvest of righteousness and peace
for those who have been trained by it.

HEBREWS 12:11

Encourage one another and build each other up.

1 THESSALONIANS 5:11

ountain climbers will often step back from a particularly difficult overhang or stretch and discuss how to surmount it. Much of the fun in the sport is encountering the challenges and figuring out a way to get around them. If mountain climbing were easy, it would lose a great deal of its appeal.

Our relationships can be looked at the same way. Instead of immediately thinking about how we can take a helicopter to the top, we might take a climber's approach and think, "This is really tough. This is a challenge, no doubt about it. How do I keep loving this person in the face of this challenge?"

Ask yourself this question: Would I rather live a life of ease and comfort and remain immature in Christ, or am I willing to be seasoned with suffering if by doing so I am conformed to the image of Christ?

I t is unrealistic to assume that the initial pledge of marital fidelity will be an "easy" one to keep. The reason we promise to love each other "till death do us part" is precisely because our society knows that such a promise will be sorely tried—otherwise, the promise wouldn't be necessary! We don't make public promises that we will regularly nourish our bodies with food or buy ourselves adequate clothing.

Everyone who enters the marriage relationship will come to a point where the marriage starts to "rub" somewhat adversely. It is *for these times* that the promise is made. Anticipating struggle, God has ordained a remedy, holding us to our word of commitment.

In this struggle we become nobler people. There are numerous areas in which both you and I can continue to grow. Nobility, sacrifice, and unselfishness are just a few.

TO MAKE HER HOLY

*Husbands, love your wives, just as Christ loved the church
and gave himself up for her to make her holy.*

EPHESIANS 5:25 – 26

Please don't resent it when your spouse brings up an area that really *does*
need to be addressed. We become blinded to our faults all too easily,
and our spouses, who know us best, can lovingly point them out.

God calls believers to grow in righteousness: "You were taught,
with regard to your former way of life, to put off your old self, which
is being corrupted by its deceitful desires; to be made new in the
attitude of your minds; and to put on the new self, created to be like
God in true righteousness and holiness" (Ephesians 4:22 – 24).

If your spouse is a believer, she or he is your sister or brother
in Christ; as fellow believers, we're called to encourage each other to
grow in character.

A heavyweight boxing champion who dodges all serious contenders to consistently fight marshmallows is ridiculed. Christians who dodge all serious struggle and seek to put themselves in whatever situations and relationships are easiest are doing the same thing—they're coasting, and eventually that coasting will define them and—even worse—shape them.

If there's one thing young engaged couples need to hear, it's that *a good marriage is not something you find, it's something you work for.* It takes struggle. You must crucify your selfishness. You must at times confront, and at other times confess. The practice of forgiveness is essential.

This is undeniably hard work! But eventually it pays off. Eventually, it creates a relationship of beauty, trust, and mutual support.

Don't run from the struggles of marriage. Embrace them. Grow in them. Draw nearer to God because of them. Through them you will reflect more of the spirit of Jesus Christ.

The connection one can make between Abraham Lincoln's marriage and his mission is not difficult. It is easy to see how a man who might quit on a difficult marriage would not have the character to hold together a crumbling nation. Lincoln was virtually obsessed with saving the Union; what better training ground than the difficult marriage that required such tenacity from him?

Not only did Lincoln's difficult marriage not deter him from achieving greatness, one might argue that it actually helped prepare him for greatness. Lincoln's character was tested and refined on a daily basis so that when the true test came, he was able to stand strong.

Perhaps Lincoln's example can set us free from the notion that a difficult marriage will hold us back rather than prepare us for our life's work; maybe he can deliver us from the bondage of seeking tension-free lives over building lives of meaning and character.

Teaches Us to Forgive

Many years ago, I and a few close friends celebrated our high school graduation by hiking on Mount Rainier. Before I attempted to jump a fast-moving creek, one of my friends advised me, "Just make sure you fall forward." The advice was well heeded. Even if I didn't make the jump, as long as I kept my momentum going forward, I wouldn't be swept into the stream.

Christian marriage is also about learning to fall forward. Obstacles arise, anger flares up, and weariness dulls our feelings and our senses. When this happens, the spiritually immature respond by pulling back, becoming more distant from their spouse, or even seeking to start over with somebody "more exciting." Yet maturity is reached by continuing to move forward past the pain and apathy. Falls are inevitable. We can't control that, but we can control the direction in which we fall—toward or away from our spouse.

This call to "fall forward" puts the focus on initiating intimacy. We cheapen marriage if we reduce it to nothing more than a negative "I agree to never have sex with anyone else." Marriage points to a gift of self that goes well beyond sexual fidelity. Mary Anne Oliver calls it an "interpenetration of being." Getting married is agreeing to grow together, into each other, to virtually commingle our souls so that we share a unique and rare bond.

Communication is the blood of marriage that carries vital oxygen into the heart of our romance. Along with verbal communication comes physical communication—the act of touching. This includes sexual expression, but also nonsexual touch.

Interpenetration of souls is a *duty* incumbent on every husband and wife. Some of us naturally gravitate toward the desire for sex, and some toward verbal communication. We have a duty to meet our spouse in their need.

The spiritual discipline embedded in learning to fall forward can be described as the "discipline of fellowship." In addition to the more general nature of pursuit, this discipline is further nurtured through three spiritual practices: learning not to run from conflict, learning how to compromise, and learning to accept others.

Yet another spiritual discipline of fellowship—in fact, one of the most difficult spiritual disciplines of all—is the discipline of forgiveness.

The more enterprising among us might attempt to use our spouse's sin as an excuse to pull back, but this is hardly a Christian response, because *all* of us sin against each other. In fact, one of marriage's primary purposes is to teach us how to forgive. This spiritual discipline provides us with the power we need to keep falling forward in the context of a sinful world.

Jesus said,
"[Father], forgive us our sins,
for we also forgive everyone who sins against us."

LUKE 11:4

Jesus said,
"Do not judge, and you will not be judged.
Do not condemn, and you will not be condemned.
Forgive, and you will be forgiven."

LUKE 6:37

Paul writes that "no one will be declared righteous in [God's] sight by observing the law" (Romans 3:20). Our spouses will never achieve a "lawful" sinlessness. It just won't happen. We will be sinned against and we will be hurt. When that happens, we'll have a choice to make: We can give in to our hurt, resentment, and bitterness, or we can grow as a Christian and learn yet another important lesson on how to forgive.

Paul goes on to say that "now a righteousness from God, *apart from law*, has been made known" (Romans 3:21, italics added). It's a righteousness based on the "redemption that came by Christ Jesus" and on "faith" (Romans 3:24, 27).

None of us can live up to the law; all of us will break it. Marriage teaches us—indeed, practically forces us—to learn to live by extending grace and forgiveness to people who have sinned against us.

❋

We can give in to our hurt,

resentment, and bitterness,

or we can grow as a Christian and learn

yet another important lesson

on how to forgive.

❋

One time I spoke at a staff retreat for an Episcopalian church at a Roman Catholic lay order's retreat center. The chapel was very small but very distinguished, and I poked around a little, shortly after I arrived. I saw a confessional in the back so I opened the door and was startled to find, of all things, a file cabinet.

Sometimes that's what marriage is like: Our spouse has confessed sins and weaknesses to us, and we've kept every confession in a mental file cabinet, ready to be taken out and used in our defense or in an attack. But true forgiveness is a process, not an event. It is rarely the case that we are able to forgive "one time" and the matter is settled. Far more often, we must relinquish our bitterness a dozen times or more, continually choosing to release the offender from our judgment.

THE PREYER

Be self-controlled and alert. Your enemy the devil prowls around like a roaring lion looking for someone to devour.

1 PETER 5:8

A married couple's relationship is the inner fortress in a cosmic spiritual battle. This fortress is not limited to just a man and woman; it also protects the children who result from that union.

With so much at stake, can we afford to be lackadaisical? Dare we forget that a powerful, pernicious being has made it his aim to wreck what God is trying to build? Even worse, are we cooperating with his agenda? By our actions (refusing to forgive, holding a grudge, neglecting to build spiritual intimacy), are we putting our marriages at risk?

Ask God to give you a forgiving heart, a loving heart, and a pure heart. Keep moving toward your spouse. Guard what God has given you.

The key to the discipline of fellowship is understanding this fundamental reality: All of us face struggles, and each one of us is currently facing a struggle that we're having less than 100 percent success overcoming. If we're married, the fact is we're also married to someone who is failing in some way.

We can respond to this "bitter juice" by becoming bitter people, or we can use it as a spiritual discipline and transform its exercise into the honey of a holy life. In this fallen world, struggles, sin, and unfaithfulness are a given. The only question is whether our response to these struggles, sin, and unfaithfulness will draw us closer to God—or whether it will estrange us from ourselves, our Creator, and each other.

Will we fall forward, or will we fall away?

Teaches Us to Serve

Paul calls us to emulate Christ Jesus, who, though he was "in very nature God, ... made himself nothing, taking the very nature of a servant" (Philippians 2:6–7).

It's precisely this servant call that makes marriage so beneficial spiritually—and so difficult personally. When I asked my wife to marry me, I was just twenty-two years old. My decision was based almost entirely on what I thought she would bring to the marriage. She looked good; we had fun together; she loved the Lord. And my suspicion is that her thoughts were running in the same direction: Can this guy support me? Do I find him attractive? Would he be a good father?

These aren't bad questions to ask, but once the ceremony is over, if we want to enter a truly Christian marriage, we have to turn 180 degrees and ask ourselves, "How can I serve my mate?"

95

In 1998, I gave an evangelistic talk at a university. The most scandalous thing I said in the mind of one student was when I talked about "mutual submission." Some of the students were so inundated with "look out for number one" that the thought of submitting to anybody was as radical as anything they had ever heard. "Sacrifice" and "relationship" simply did not belong in the same sentence as far as they were concerned.

Marriage creates a situation in which our desire to be served and coddled can be replaced with a more noble desire to serve others—even to sacrifice for others. The beauty of marriage is that it confronts our selfishness and demands our service twenty-four hours a day. When we're most tired, most worn down, and feeling more sorry for ourselves than ever, we have the opportunity to confront feelings of self-pity by getting up and serving our mate.

Marriage creates a situation

in which our desire to be served and coddled

can be replaced with a more noble desire

to serve others — even to sacrifice for others.

Our motivations for marrying often are selfish. But my desire is to reclaim marriage as one of the most selfless states a Christian can enter.

To fully sanctify the marital relationship, we must live it together as Jesus lived his life—embracing the discipline of sacrifice and service *as a daily practice*. In the same way that Jesus gave his body for us, we're to lay down our energy, our bodies, and our lives for others.

Kathleen and Thomas Hart refer to the "paschal mystery" of marriage—the process of dying and rising as a pattern of life for married people. Each day we must die to our own desires and rise as a servant. Each day we're called to identify with the suffering Christ on the cross, and then be empowered by the resurrected Christ. We die to our expectations, our demands, and our fears. We rise to compromise, service, and courage.

God is always worthy of being obeyed and served, so when I act out of obedience to him, the person who receives my service doesn't have to be deserving—they're benefiting from what I owe *God*. Yes, this truth is hard to apply in marriage, where demands and expectations are so plentiful, but I try to remind myself of this fact: God is always worthy of being obeyed, and God calls me to serve my spouse—so regardless of how she treats me at any particular moment, I am called to respond as a servant.

Jesus' example has challenged me greatly in this regard. *None* of the disciples deserved to have their feet washed at the Last Supper—all of them would abandon him within a few hours— yet Jesus went ahead and did it anyway (see John 13:1–17).

GOOD IN BED

I have become in his eyes
like one bringing contentment.

SONG OF SONGS 8:10

Honestly ask yourself, "Am I good in bed?" On the day we marry, we gain a monopoly of sorts. Our spouses commit to have sexual relations with no one else. The only intimate life our spouses can and will enjoy is the intimate life we choose to give them. Regardless of whether we act thoughtfully, creatively, or selfishly in bed, they receive *only* what we provide.

Rather than make us careless, this exclusivity should make us grateful, and therefore even more eager to please our mates. The principle goes well beyond the bedroom, of course. You're the primary person for intimate talk and encouragement. Are you "good in communication" too? You're the first person who should be supporting your spouse in prayer. Are you "good in prayer"?

Another aspect of true service is that it's performed willingly. A begrudging, complaining service is not a Christian one.

I've learned to guard not just my servant's actions, but my servant's *spirit*. If I serve Lisa with little puffs of exasperation, grunting every time I lift a finger on her behalf, I'm exhibiting a proud, false-martyr's spirit, not the attitude of Jesus Christ.

I go back to imagining the scene that day as Jesus washed Judas's feet. Do you think Jesus was especially rough as he scrubbed Judas's toes? Do you think he maybe gave Judas's ankle a little twist, just enough to let him know that he knew what was about to happen? I don't think so.

We're not just after the imitation of Christ's *actions* in our home. We also want to model Christ's *spirit* and *attitude*.

There is true joy when true service is offered up with a true heart.

I will be most fulfilled as a Christian when I use everything I have—including my money and time—as a way to serve others, with my spouse getting first priority (after God). This commitment absolutely undercuts petty power games. If I humiliate my wife by pointing out how much more important I am to the family's financial well-being, or if she points out how utterly helpless I am in doing certain domestic chores, we don't just cheapen each other; we cheapen ourselves. We destroy the entire notion of Christian fellowship by denying that every part has its place in the body of Christ (1 Corinthians 12:14–31).

These little acts of sacrifice will not always be rewarded or even noticed by our spouse. But if we guard our hearts from bitterness and resentment, we will receive affirmation where it counts and where it means the most—from our heavenly Father.

Promotes Spiritual Growth through Sexuality

If sex is going to turn us toward God and each other, it is vital that we examine it with Christian understanding. Christian spirituality serves us in at least three ways here: It teaches us the goodness of sex while reminding us that there are things that are more important than sex. It allows us to experience pleasure without making pleasure the idol of our existence. It teaches us that sex can certainly season our lives but also reminds us that sex will never fully nourish our souls.

To begin to view sex in this positive sense, as a mirror of our desire and passion for God, the institution of marriage becomes all-important. If we think about sex *only within the confines of marriage*—thereby sanctifying it as God intended it—the analogy of sex leading us toward God may not seem so far-fetched.

We Christians can learn a thing or two from the Jewish foundations of our faith. To the ancient Jew, nothing was more important than the preservation and purity of the family line. Progeny was how the unpolluted, God-chosen race would continue. Yet Jewish views about sex went beyond procreation.

The ancient Jewish text *The Holy Letter* (written by Nahmanides in the thirteenth century) sees sex as a mystical experience of meeting with God: "Through the act [of intercourse] they become partners with God in the act of creation. This is the mystery of what the sages said, 'When a man unites with his wife in holiness, the Shekinah is between them in the mystery of man and woman.'" The breadth of this statement is sobering when you consider that this *shekinah* glory is the same presence experienced by Moses when God met with him face-to-face (see Exodus 24:15–18).

Once we evaluate the theological foundations on which we build our view of marital sex, we also need to examine our emotional attitudes. In this case, gratitude must replace guilt.

A young man became involved in a satanic cult whose liturgy focused on the compositions of Bach. He later became a Christian and started attending a local church. When the organist played a piece composed by Bach, the young believer was overcome by fear and fled.

Sex is that way for some Christians. They try hard not to believe that sex is inherently evil, but because of previous negative experiences, to them it *feels* evil.

If guilt rather than gratitude casts a shadow over your experience of sex, practice thanking God for what sex involves. This can sanctify an act that all-too-many Christians divorce from their spiritual life with God.

For this reason a man will leave his father and mother
and be united to his wife, and the two will become one flesh."
This is a profound mystery —
but I am talking about Christ and the church.

EPHESIANS 5:31 – 32

Like an apple tree among the trees of the forest
    is my lover among the young men.
I delight to sit in his shade,
    and his fruit is sweet to my taste.
He has taken me to the banquet hall,
    and his banner over me is love.

SONG OF SONGS 2:3 – 4

During my engagement to Lisa, I gave her a poem titled "My Sister, His Bride," in which I talked about how the step we were taking toward marriage was so monumental in this world, but that there already existed a more significant eternal bond between us that would outlive our status as husband and wife: brother and sister in Christ.

While physical pleasure is good and acceptable, we mustn't reduce sex to a merely *physical* experience. It is about more — much more — than that. Sex speaks of spiritual realities far more profound than mere pleasure.

When Paul tells us that our bodies are temples of the Holy Spirit (1 Corinthians 6:19), our contemplations on the significance of sex take on an entirely new meaning. In a Christian marriage, these are *sanctified* bodies; bodies in which God is present through his Holy Spirit; bodies coming together, celebrating, but in a spirit of reverence and holiness.

assion is a fearful thing to some. It's frightening to want God. What if he doesn't show up? It's even scarier to want another human. What if they spurn our advances or use our desire against us?

This provides an avenue of spiritual growth. We can use this sense of need as a way to grow as servants of each other. In a healthy Christian marriage in which both husband and wife lovingly seek to fulfill the sexual desires of each other, both can learn that God will minister to them as well. Just as Jesus uses the example (Matthew 7:9) of an earthly father who won't give his son a stone when he asks for bread—and encourages his followers to likewise trust God to give good gifts—so a man or woman may be able to open up their heart to God when they experience their spouse's generosity in meeting their need for sexual expression.

In a healthy Christian marriage

in which both husband and wife lovingly seek

to fulfill the sexual desires of each other,

both can learn that God

will minister to them as well.

Marriage takes the raw force of sexuality and connects it with emotional intimacy, companionship, family responsibilities, and permanency of relationship. In so doing, it provides a context that encourages spiritual growth by moving us to value character, virtue, and godliness over against an idealized physical form.

Jesus' disciple Peter says, quite explicitly, that women shouldn't focus on an external beauty that requires "outward adornment," but instead aspire after a beauty "of your inner self, the unfading beauty of a gentle and quiet spirit, which is of great worth in God's sight" (1 Peter 3:3–4).

I'm convinced that, with God's Spirit within us, we can become enamored with the things that enamor God. By denying myself errant appetites and by meditating and feeding on the right things—including being "captivated" by my wife's love (Proverbs 5:18–19)—I will train myself to desire only what is proper to be desired.

God is worthy of infinite celebration, and marital sexuality provides a unique context for celebration. Naked in each other's arms, it doesn't matter if you have a portfolio worth a million dollars or if you're struggling with the realities of a negative net worth. You could be delighting in a honeymoon as you celebrate life in your twenties or thirties, or renewing your passion as you celebrate life in your sixties or seventies. Regardless of your status in life, you're celebrating a deeply human dance, a transcendent experience created by no less a preeminent mind than that of Almighty God himself.

The marriage relationship makes available to us a full, responsive, and responsible human experience—assuming responsibility, to be sure, but along with that responsibility relishing the very real and earthy pleasure of sexual activity, an intense celebration that gently reminds us of the heavenly existence that awaits all God's children.

Makes Us Aware
of God's Presence

It was the pursuit of God's presence that sent so many men and women into monasteries and convents. These earnest souls believed that they could best experience the delight of God's presence by engaging in a life free from the encumbrances of earning a living and caring for a family. Although ancient religious orders differed substantially, most often a monk's or nun's life was structured around this constant awareness of God. The day began and ended with prayer, there were often long periods of enforced silence, and the community itself created an environment that encouraged its citizens to look heavenward.

How can we, as married saints, use the daily rush of activities and the seeming chaos of family life as a reminder of God's presence? To be sure, we have many challenges to overcome, but isn't there a way we can use marriage to *draw* us to God?

Jesus said, "Where two or three come together in my name, there am I with them" (Matthew 18:20). The family that will enjoy Jesus' presence as a customary part of their union is a family that is joined precisely because husband and wife want to invite Jesus into the deeper parts of their marriage. They are not coming together in order to escape loneliness, more favorably pool their financial resources, or merely gain an outlet for sexual desire. Above all these other reasons, they have joined themselves to each other as a way to live out and deepen their faith in God.

Even if you didn't enter marriage for this reason, you can make a decision to *maintain* your marriage on this basis. The day you do this, you will find that marriage can be a favorable funnel to direct God's presence into your daily life.

God has said,
"Never will I leave you;
never will I forsake you."

HEBREWS 13:5

Where can I go from your Spirit?
Where can I flee from your presence?
If I go up to the heavens, you are there;
if I make my bed in the depths, you are there.
If I rise on the wings of the dawn,
if I settle on the far side of the sea,
even there your hand will guide me,
your right hand will hold me fast.

PSALM 139:7 – 10

Just as the silence of the Trappist monks is a discipline designed to draw them into the realm of the holy, so the conversation of marriage can bend us toward God.

In marriage, it is our duty to communicate. To be sure, every marriage needs times of silence and meditation. But in our relationship with our spouse, communication is a discipline of love. Our reaching out to each other mirrors God reaching out to us, and as he does so, his presence and character become better known to us. God loves us with words; we can love our spouses with those same words and grow more like Christ in the process.

Communication calls us out of ourselves. Learning how to do this is as much a prerequisite for building a meaningful prayer life as it is for building a meaningful marriage. The act of communication invites God's presence into our daily existence.

THE MINISTRY OF NOTICING

O LORD, you have searched me
and you know me.
You know when I sit and when I rise;
you perceive my thoughts from afar.
You discern my going out and my lying down;
you are familiar with all my ways.

PSALM 139:1–3

When Paul tells husbands we're supposed to love our wives like Christ loves the church (Ephesians 5:25), for one thing, he's telling us we're supposed to *notice* them. Everyone else may take them for granted, but it's our job to take the time to notice and affirm them.

Wives, you can do this as well. You can replenish our souls by simply noticing your husbands and telling them what you're thinking.

Some of my most intimate moments with my heavenly Father come when I realize he's watching, he's noticing, he's getting it all down.

Loving begins with noticing. A spiritually discerning marriage will be a tool of sanctification. As we look at our spouse, we are reminded of God's presence and image. And in the presence of God, we long to become more holy. Hebrews 12:14 says, "Make every effort to live in peace with all men and to be holy; without holiness no one will see the Lord."

It's no easy discipline, this cooperating in sanctification. My tendency is to *hide* my faults rather than work on trying to transform them. Every day I'm choosing to either spend my energy covering up my mistakes and trying to create a false, glittering image, or I'm repenting and cooperating with God to become a more holy person. Living with a woman made in the image of God calls me to honesty and to growth in sanctification—*provided I allow my marriage to remind me of God's presence and his claims on my life.*

As we look at our spouse,

we are reminded of God's presence and image.

And in the presence of God,

we long to become more holy.

Marriage, on its own, should not and does not make it difficult to pursue God and enjoy his presence. What makes spirituality in marriage difficult is a laissez-faire attitude within marriage. When we don't seek to communicate; when we ignore the divine ache in our soul and try to soothe that ache with human companionship alone; when we fail to behold the image of God in our spouse and instead embark on a deceitful life; when we become disengaged as married people and do not revel in marriage's call to live meaningful, productive lives — *this* is what can lead us ultimately to separation from God.

In many ways, marriage is a slippery slope. If we're not vigilant, we'll fall backwards. But if we enter marriage thoughtfully, purposefully, and with godly intentions, our wedlock will shape us in a way that few other life experiences can. It will usher us into God's own presence.

❀

Develops Our Sense of Purpose

The intimacy of the marriage relationship is something most of us desire, but how do we enter this union without sacrificing our sense of personal mission before God? How do we promise to be unreservedly faithful toward our spouse when we've already pledged to be unreservedly available for God's service?

It's not easy to balance the competing demands of an intense human relationship and an overarching spiritual devotion. One of the great challenges of marriage is maintaining a sense of individual mission while living in a cooperative relationship.

Being married brings obligations—some particularly intense ones for those who are by nature ambitious. At times I must sacrifice my ambition to succeed in God's service so I can be fully present and involved in the lives of my wife and children. The tension should lead us to ask the question, "If I ignore God's daughter [God's son] to do God's work, am I honoring God?"

One of the great challenges of marriage is the seemingly endless tasks that accompany married life. How can I experience peace and serenity, focus on the presence of God, and devote myself to worship when the lawn needs to be mowed, the garbage needs to be taken out, the kids want time alone with me....

To a woman with this same concern, Francis De Sales wrote, "I remember you telling me how much the multiplicity of your affairs weighs on you. [This] is a good opportunity for acquiring the true and solid virtues."

De Sales wrote with the wonderful assumption that the more difficult something is, the more spiritually beneficial it will be, as it builds our character. It's only natural when facing all these responsibilities that our souls cry out for relief. But Francis urges us to draw maximum benefit from them by crying out for patience and virtue and growth in Christlikeness.

We have different gifts, according to the grace given us.
If a man's gift is prophesying, let him use it in proportion to
his faith. If it is serving, let him serve;
if it is teaching, let him teach; if it is encouraging,
let him encourage; if it is contributing to the needs of others,
let him give generously; if it is leadership, let him
govern diligently; if it is showing mercy, let him do it cheerfully.

ROMANS 12:6–8

It was [Christ] who gave some to be apostles, some
to be prophets, some to be evangelists, and some to be pastors
and teachers, to prepare God's people for works of service.

EPHESIANS 4:11–12

A married woman once wrote Francis De Sales to express her concern that her marital and spiritual devotion were at conflict. He dismissed this concern out of hand, encouraging her, "Let us be what we are, and let us be it well." In other words, if we are married, we are married, and we must not try to live as if we were otherwise. Francis noted that by living with this attitude, we "do honor to the Master whose work we are."

De Sales did not view marriage as a compromise to our mission before God, precisely because if we are led into marriage, then marriage *becomes* an essential element of our mission—not our *only* mission, to be sure, but at least the front lines from which our mission is launched.

A spiritually alive marriage

will remain a marriage of two individuals

in pursuit of a common vision

outside themselves.

When marriage becomes our primary pursuit, our delight in the relationship will be crippled by fear, possessiveness, and self-centeredness. We were made to admire, respect, and love someone who has a purpose bigger than ourselves, a purpose centered on God's untiring work of calling his people home to his heart of love.

We allow marriage to point beyond itself when we accept two central missions: becoming the people God created us to be, and doing the work God has given us to do. If we embrace — not just accept, but actively *embrace* — these two missions, we will have a full life, a rich life, a meaningful life, and a successful life. The irony is, we will probably also have a happy marriage, but that will come as a blessed by-product of putting everything else in order.

There's another challenge when two believers are both committed to pursuing a deeper spiritual reality in marriage—the formidable task of working to become not just a holy spouse, but a holy couple.

Christian spirituality throughout the history of the church has undeniably been focused on a solitary pursuit of God. This emphasis needs to change. Most of the church serve God within a family relationship; it stands to reason that 90 percent of the teaching regarding the spiritual life should thus be placed in a marital context.

What if a few Christian couples made it their goal to become a "couple-saint"? No longer defining their relationship to God in solitary terms but working together to present themselves as a holy unit?

It is, at the very least, an interesting invitation. Is there anyone who will take up that invitation for today—for such a time as this?

ALSO AVAILABLE
Sacred Marriage
Softcover
ISBN 978-0-310-24282-6
$12.99 US/£7.99/$16.49 Cdn

Devotions for a Sacred Marriage
Jacketed Hardcover
ISBN 978-0-310-25595-6
$14.99 US/8.99/$18.99 Cdn

Sacred Influence
Jacketed Hardcover
ISBN 978-0-310-24740-1
$19.99 US/£11.99/$24.99 Cdn

At Inspirio, we would love to hear your stories and your feedback.
Please send your comments to us by way of email at
icares@zondervan.com or to the address below:

inspirio

Attn: Inspirio Cares
5300 Patterson Avenue SE
Grand Rapids, MI 49530

If you would like further information about Inspirio
and the products we create, please visit us at:
www.inspiriogifts.com

Thank you and God bless!